2 Practice Tests
for the
OLSAT®
Grade 3 (4th Grade Entry)
LEVEL D

MW00594229

Copyright© 2019 by Origins Publications

Written and Edited by: Gifted and Talented Test Prep Team

ISBN: 978-1-948255-54-7

The Otis Lennon School Ability Test (OLSAT®) is a registered trademark of NCS Pearson, which is not affiliated with Origins Publications. NCS Pearson has not endorsed the contents of this book.

Origins Publications, New York, NY, USA

ABOUT ORIGINS PUBLICATIONS

Origins Publications helps students develop their higher-order thinking skills while also improving their chances of admission into gifted and accelerated learner programs.

Our goal is to unleash and nurture the genius in every student. We do this by offering educational and test prep materials that are fun, challenging and provide a sense of accomplishment.

Please contact us with any questions.
info@originspublications.com

Contents

PREPARATION GUIDE

Part 1. Introduction to the OLSAT®-D

The Otis Lennon School Ability Test® (OLSAT®) is an important exam; the more you know about it, the better you will fare. This guide offers an overview of the types of questions that are likely to be on the test, some test-taking strategies to improve performance during preparation and on test day, and sample OLSAT tests that students can use to test their knowledge and practice their test-taking skills.

Why the OLSAT-D?

Many gifted and talented programs and highly-selective public schools across the USA require students to pass an exam in order to be admitted to the school or program. The OLSAT-D is often used as an assessment tool or admissions test in 3rd grade for entry into 4th grade of highly-competitive programs and schools.

Who Takes The OLSAT-D?

Third graders who want to gain admission to fourth grade gifted and talented program or highly-selective school. The OLSAT-D can also be used as an assessment tool by teachers to decipher which students would benefit from an accelerated or remedial curriculum.

When Does the OLSAT Take Place?

This depends on the school district you reside in, or want to attend. Check with the relevant school/district to learn more about test dates and the application/registration process.

OLSAT Level D Overview

The OLSAT is a test of abstract thinking and an individual's ability to reason logically. It measures verbal, quantitative, and spatial reasoning ability. In taking the OLSAT, students will be evaluated on their ability to perceive information accurately, understand relationships and patterns among objects, reason through abstract problems, apply generalizations, and recall and evaluate information.

The OLSAT covers topics that students may not see in school, so children will need to think a little differently in order to do well. A student's stress management and time management skills are also tested during the nearly hour-long exam.

Length

The OLSAT Level D test is a 50-minute test.

Format

Each test is made up of 64 multiple choice questions. The questions are distributed as follows:

VERBAL		NONVERBAL	
Verbal Comprehension		**Figural Reasoning**	
Antonyms	4	Figural Analogies	6
Sentence Arrangement	4	Figural Series	4
Sentence Completion	4	Pattern Matrix	4
Verbal Reasoning		Figural Classifications	6
Arithmetic Reasoning	4	**Quantitative Reasoning**	
Logical Selection	4	Numeric Inferences	4
Verbal Analogies	4	Number Matrix	4
Verbal Classification	4	Numeric Series	4
Word/letter matrix	4		
		TOTAL QUESTIONS	64

Test Sections

The test consists of verbal material and nonverbal material. The verbal material consists of verbal comprehension and verbal reasoning questions, while the nonverbal material consists of figural reasoning and quantitative reasoning questions.

Verbal Material

VERBAL COMPREHENSION QUESTIONS

The verbal comprehension questions are aimed at measuring students' ability to gather and manipulate information from language. In particular, these questions seek to evaluate how students understand the way words and sentences relate to each other, and also how students interpret nuances in language.

There are three types of verbal comprehension questions:

✓ **Antonyms:** These questions require students to search for the opposite meaning of a given word within the answer choices provided. In particular, this group of questions aims to evaluate a student's vocabulary skills. Ultimately, these questions require a sophisticated understanding of vocabulary because students have to not only comprehend a word, but also understand it enough so that they can recognize its true opposite.

✓ **Sentence Arrangement**: These questions provide students with sentences that have been mixed up. Looking at this jumbled set of words, students must piece the words together to compose a complete thought. These questions assess a student's ability to understand the structure of language by asking them to take fragmented parts and, from them, create a whole.

✓ **Sentence Completion**: With these questions students will have to "fill in the blank(s)." The answer options outline a number of words that could be used to complete a given sentence. However, students must choose the words that create a complete, logical sentence.

VERBAL REASONING QUESTIONS

The verbal reasoning component of the test measures a student's ability to comprehend patterns, relationships, and context clues in writing in order to solve a problem. In order to be successful in answering these questions, students must be able to fully understand what a question is asking, as well as make inferences based on what they have read.

The verbal reasoning questions on the test are composed of five different question types:

✓ **Arithmetic Reasoning**: These verbal problems incorporate mathematical reasoning. Some questions assess basic concepts, including counting, and estimation. Others assess more sophisticated concepts such as reasoning and solving word problems. The main skill tested here is the ability to create mathematical problems from language and to solve those problems.

✓ **Logical Selection**: In order to find the answers to these questions, students have to apply logical reasoning to uncover the best answer. These questions often asks students to consider which answer *might* be correct, versus which answer options are *always* correct. Being able to make that distinction is key.

✓ **Verbal Analogies:** These questions ask students to consider the relationship between a pair of words, then apply this relationship to another pair of words. Students' ability to correctly uncover these relationships is key to answering these type of questions.

✓ **Verbal Classification**: With these questions, students must look at a series of words or concepts and identify which one does not fit with the others. In answering this type of question, students must be able to evaluate the relationships among words.

✓ **Word/letter Matrices**: These questions provide students with a matrix of letters or words. Students must perceive the pattern or relationship among these words in order to supply a missing letter or word.

Non-Verbal Material
FIGURAL REASONING QUESTIONS

The purpose of these questions is to measure a student's ability to reason their way through non-language based scenarios. These questions take a more visual format than the verbal questions, incorporating geometric figures instead of words. Students will be expected to find the relationship between numbers or objects in a pattern, to predict and create what the next level of the pattern will look like, and generalize the rules they discover.

There are four figural reasoning question types:

✓ **Figural Analogies**: Like verbal analogies, these questions require students to identify the relationship of a given pair. With these questions, however, students are asked to examine the relationship between figures instead of words. Once students have uncovered this relationship, they then must apply this rule to a second pair of figures. This question type assesses the student's ability to infer a relationship between a pair of geometric shapes and select the shape that is related to the stimulus in the same way.

✓ **Figural Classification**: In these questions, students must examine a group of figures and identify a pattern or principle that links those figures. Then, students must conclude which of the answer choices follows this same principle.

✓ **Figural Series**: With this series of questions, students must look at a series of geometric figures, discern a pattern within the series, and find the 'missing' drawing/shape in the pattern.

✓ **Pattern Matrices**: This question asks the student to supply a missing element in a matrix of geometric shapes. These questions test a student's ability to discern rules in a pattern and evaluate how those rules govern a series of geometric figures.

QUANTITATIVE REASONING QUESTIONS

These questions evaluates a student's ability to discern patterns and relationships in order to solve problems with numbers. This section requires that students be able to predict outcomes based on their knowledge of mathematics.

There are three types of quantitative reasoning questions:

✓ **Numeric Inferences**: Using computation skills, students will have to determine how two or three numbers are related. Once they have uncovered this relationship, students will have to apply this rule to another pair or trio of numbers.

✓ **Number Matrices**: For these questions, students must examine numbers in a matrix and determine what principle or rule links those numbers. Then, they must apply this rule to figure out what number should be placed in a given blank.

✓ **Numeric Series**: Students must examine a sequence of numbers and determine a pattern that governs those numbers. They will then apply that pattern in order to predict what comes next.

Part 2. Using This Book

You have made an important first step towards ensuring your student will do her best on test day by purchasing this book. This book offers general strategies your student can use to tackle the test. Your student can also prepare for the exam by taking the practice test(s) in this book.

Performance on practice tests can help identify a student's weaknesses and allow your student to focus on question types that most need to be reviewed.

When to Start Studying?

Every family/teacher and student will approach preparation for this test differently. There is no 'right' way to prepare; there is only the best way for a particular student and family/teacher. Some take the 'cram' approach, loading up on as many hours as possible before the test date. Other parents/teachers think too much focus on preparation may create anxiety in their student that could backfire on test day. In this case, a more low-key approach may work best.

With that said, repeated exposure to the format and nature of the test will help a student prepare for this challenging test. We suggest students, at minimum, take one practice test (preferably under timed conditions) and spend a minimum of 6-8 hours working through OLSAT type questions.

As they say, knowledge is power! And preparing for the OLSAT also gives students a chance to know what they are up against. This alone can help a third-grader not panic on test day when faced with unfamiliar and perplexing questions. The OLSAT measures a student's academic performance but also his ability to manage time efficiently and capacity to keep his wits under pressure.

Part 3: Exam Preparation and Test-Taking Strategies

Preparing for the OLSAT in many ways follows the same process as preparing for any other exam—your student needs to review the concepts he or she already knows and boost skills in areas that he or she is unfamiliar with. You can diagnose your student's weaknesses by analyzing her scores on the practice test in this book. Then, focus study time on reviewing and practicing more of the question types that your student finds tricky or regularly stumbles on.

General Test Taking Strategies For OLSAT Level D Test

The OLSAT® Level D does not just test your child's knowledge and skills in specific verbal and non-verbal areas, but also her test-taking skills. If your student knows the material on which she will be tested and is familiar with test-taking techniques and strategies, it will certainly improve her chances of doing well on the exam.

Help your child prepare for the test by using the following tips and strategies.

✓ KNOW THE TEST

The content and required pacing on this test is very challenging for a third grader. A student will need to sustain focus throughout the test. Because of this, it is important that your student is familiar with the format, nature and structure of the exam, and that he or she works on sample questions and takes practice tests in timed conditions.

As a general test preparation strategy, we recommend that you first review each question type with your student and ask him or her to solve practice questions without a time restriction. Then, spend time analysing the answers and explanations (both incorrect and correct for each question).

In order to succeed on the test, a student must keep calm and learn to use time wisely. That's why we recommend that students take several timed practice tests, which helps build stamina and confidence, as well as ensures that a student does not waste time on test day panicking about the unknown! A practice test also helps a student get used to reading each question carefully but quickly, and figure out the best and fastest way to transfer answers and mark the bubbles in the answer sheet. For example, practicing the simple technique of shading the bubbles quickly and efficiently can help a student gain a minute or two during the test.

Use the scores on the practice tests to identify subject areas or question types where your student is struggling. If you have limited time to prepare, spend most energy reviewing areas where your student is encountering the majority of problems.

✓ DON'T LET DIFFICULT QUESTIONS UNDERMINE CONFIDENCE

Be prepared for difficult questions on the test from the get go! The OLSAT is not given in an 'adaptive' format -- where each subsequent question increases in difficulty. The make-up of the exam is as follows; about half of the OLSAT® Level D is made up of "easy" questions, the answers to which most third graders will know. More than a third of the questions will be of medium difficulty, and students who receive close to a 'mean' score will also answer these correctly. In general, a student's strategy should be to avoid thoughtless mistakes and to solve these questions relatively quickly. About 18% of questions are difficult for most students. The students who answer some or all of these questions correctly are the ones that have the highest chance of being admitted to the assessing program or school.

So what to do when stumped with a tough question? First, a student needs to stay calm and focused. She can spend some extra time (but not too much!) on the challenging question (knowing that there are easier questions ahead which can be answered faster). If she is still unable to figure out the answer, she should make an educated guess and move on to the next question.

✓ USE PROCESS OF ELIMINATION

If a student is stumped by a question, he can use the process of elimination. Firstly, eliminate obviously wrong answers in order to narrow down the answer choices. If still in doubt after using this technique, he can make an educated guess. Process of elimination is a key technique that helps improve the probability of selecting the correct response even if a student is not sure about how to answer a question.

✓ NEVER LEAVE AN ANSWER BLANK

On the OLSAT test, no points are deducted for wrong answers. Therefore, when all else fails, educated guessing should be used as a strategy. When a student finishes the test and has time to spare, he should review the answer sheet to ensure EVERY question has a marked answer.

✓ USE TIME WISELY

The OLSAT Level D asks students to answer 64 questions in 50 minutes. On test day, a student should always be aware of the time. Scanning ahead and seeing how many questions remain in the test will help him or her gauge how much time to allocate for each question.

✓ DEVELOP FIGURAL REASONING SKILLS

On the nonverbal material, the object is to use clues to find specific patterns and relationships, and then to apply that relationship or pattern to the answer options to identify the correct one among five choices. This includes finding similarities and differences between items or sets of geometric figures, predicting the next step in a progression of geometric shapes, or supplying a missing element in a matrix. In order to improve at this aspect of the test, we suggest students spend time doing activities such as puzzles, Sudoku, chess and/or Rubik's cube, all of which help develop a child's ability to identify and interpret patterns.

✓ IMPROVE VOCABULARY & READING COMPREHENSION

The verbal material on the test is the most difficult to prep for as it requires a student to have a large vocabulary and excellent reading comprehension. This is built up over time by reading widely and analyzing what is read. If your student is preparing well enough in advance, he can spend time on building vocabulary using flashcards or, even better, learning and reviewing roots, prefixes and suffixes of words. A student can use the other general test-taking strategies to improve his score on the verbal section even if his vocabulary is not strong. However, strengthening vocabulary is a potential way to do better on the test.

✓ IGNORE ALL DISTRACTIONS

You may have tried to re-create the exact test-taking atmosphere during practice exams. But when your student goes for the real thing she will be in a room with many other children, maybe even someone with a cold who is sneezing or coughing. Tell her to ignore it all and concentrate on her test.

✓ MANAGE TEST DAY JITTERS

Avoid squeezing in a last-minute review. Instead, encourage your student to visualize his success and plan a reward for after the test is over. Encourage your student to think positive when there's a frustrating question. Freezing up and thinking all kinds of negative ideas will only kill confidence during the exam. Instead, teach your student to use positive self-talk, including "I've studied this," "I can do this," and "I can figure this problem out." If your student finds himself getting anxious, tell him to help himself relax by taking long, deep breaths. In addition, your student should eat a light, healthy breakfast, such as yogurt and granola or a low-fat, low-sugar cereal and fruit. He should dress comfortably, and wear layers so that he can take off a sweatshirt or sweater if it's too warm in the room.

✓ KEEP THINGS IN PERSPECTIVE

Yes, the OLSAT-D is an important exam, but it needs to be put in context. Perspective is important to performance. Of course your student should be serious about succeeding on the test. But she should not lose sight of other important aspects of life and become overly anxious about one test.

OLSAT® Level D
Practice Test 1

1.

Which word best completes the sentence?

A house must have _____.

A windows   **B** rugs   **C** walls   **D** stairs

2.

The words in the box go together in a certain way. Choose the word that goes where you see the question mark.

juice	pasta	?
cup	fork	spoon

A plate   **B** milk   **C** knife   **D** soup

3.

Which word best complete the sentence?

Because his shoes were untied, the boy _____ on the playground.

A ran   **B** tripped   **C** skipped   **D** walked

4.

The shapes in the boxes go together in a certain way. Which shape belongs where the question mark is?

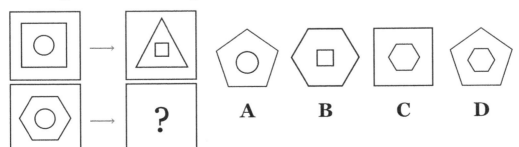

5.

If the words below were arranged to make the *best* sentence, with which letter would the <u>last</u> word of the sentence begin?

| once   a   beautiful   the   rainbow   stopped   rain   emerged |

A E   **B** S   **C** O   **D** R

6.

The numbers in the box go together in a certain way. Choose the number that goes where you see the question mark.

31	20	9
45	34	23
?	48	37

A 59   **B** 54   **C** 60   **D** 35

7.

The numbers in the box are related according to the same rule. Given this information, which number fits where the question mark is?

| 2, 4 | 1, 2 | 0, ? |

A 2   **B** 5   **C** 0   **D** 4   **E** 1

8.

The drawings in the boxes go together in a particular way. Which drawing goes where the question mark is?

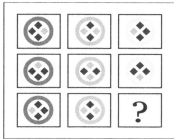

A   **B**   **C**   **D**   **E**

9.

Which number comes next in the series?

| 2 | 7 | 12 | 17 | 22 | 27 | ? |

A 29   **B** 37   **C** 42   **D** 32   **E** 31

10.

The opposite of *absent* is _____

A attendance   **B** dismiss   **C** present   **D** arrival

11.

The third grade is having a pizza party. Ms Coons ordered eleven pizzas. Mr Rogers ordered eight less pizzas than Ms Coons. How many pizzas did Mr Rogers order?

A 5   **B** 4   **C** 3   **D** 2

12.

The figures in the boxes below relate to each other in a particular way. Which figure from the answer choices belongs in the box with a question mark?

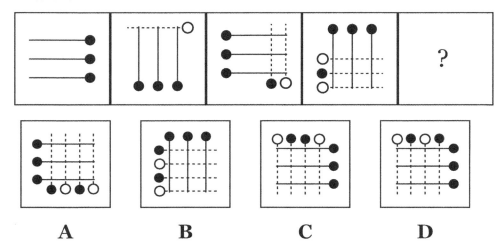

   A   **B**   **C**   **D**

13.

candle : wax as window :

A door   **B** fabric   **C** open   **D** glass

14.

Which word does *not* go with the others?

A question mark   **B** comma   **C** period   **D** exclamation point   **E** sentence

15.

The figures below relate to each other in a particular way. One of them doesn't belong. Which figure does not belong with the others?

 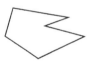

A   **B**   **C**   **D**   **E**

16.

Which word best completes the sentence?
All libraries must have _____.

A computers   **B** chairs   **C** shelves   **D** books

17.

The words in the box go together in a certain way. Choose the word that goes where you see the question mark.

py	co	copy
th	ma	?

A am **B** math **C** coma **D** them

18.

Which words best complete the sentence?

Although the math assessment was very _____, Josie _____ until she finished.

A easy, rushed **B** challenging, rushed **C** difficult, persevered **D** easy, persevered

19.

The shapes in the top boxes go together in a certain way. Which shape belongs where the question mark is?

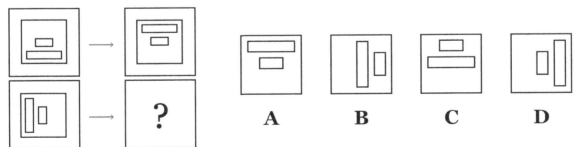

A **B** **C** **D**

20.

If the words below were arranged to make the *best* sentence, with which letter would the <u>last</u> word of the sentence begin?

sides polygons are of four quadrilaterals composed

A Q **B** P **C** S **D** C

21.

The numbers in the box go together in a certain way. Choose the number that goes where you see the question mark.

41	39	37
46	44	42
51	49	?

A 52 **B** 32 **C** 47 **D** 57

22.

The numbers in the box are related according to the same rule. Given this information, which number fits where the question mark is?

21, 10	31, 20	41, ?

A 20 **B** 30 **C** 52 **D** 14 **E** 40

23.

The drawings in the boxes go together in a particular way. Which drawing goes where the question mark is?

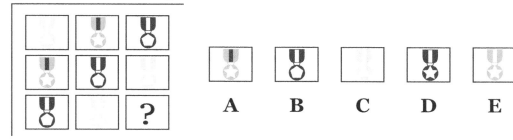

A   **B**   **C**   **D**   **E**

24.

Which number comes next in the series?

40   34   28   22   16   10   ?

A 6 **B** 4 **C** 16 **D** 8 **E** 2

25.

The opposite of *scarce* is _____.

A abundant   **B** brave   **C** more   **D** hoard

26.

Omar has 11 boxes of chocolate. He gave away all of the boxes except 5 boxes. How many boxes does Omar have left?

A 16   **B** 6   **C** 5   **D** 9

27.

The figures in the boxes below relate to each other in a particular way. Which figure from the answer choices belongs in the box with a question mark?

A   **B**   **C**   **D**

28.

dog : mammal as frog :

A slimy   **B** amphibian   **C** reptile   **D** animal

29.

Which word does not go with the others?

A cockpit   **B** engine   **C** wheels   **D** plane   **E** wings

30.

The figures below relate to each other in a particular way. One of them doesn't belong. Which figure does not belong?

A   **B**   **C**   **D**   **E**

31.

An ecosystem must have _____.

A fish   **B** plants   **C** humans   **D** mountains

32.

The words in the box go together in a certain way. Choose the word that goes where you see the question mark.

ba	tch	batch
ba	ste	?

A basin   **B** bates   **C** bails   **D** baste

33.

Which words best complete the sentence?

Mrs. Barry is a _____ teacher, so she doesn't _____ misconduct.

A strict, tolerate   **B** nice, create   **C** negative, avoid   **D** pleasant, question

34.

The shapes in the top boxes go together in a certain way. Which shape belongs where the question mark is?

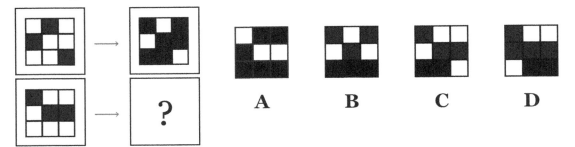

35.

If the words below were arranged to make the *best* sentence, with which letter would the **first** word of the sentence begin.

| river | a | woods | dense | the | calm | through | meandered |

A W   **B** R   **C** T   **D** A

36.

The numbers in the box go together in a certain way. Choose the number that goes where you see the question mark.

16	19	23
19	22	26
22	?	29

A 15   **B** 25   **C** 26   **D** 24

37.

The numbers in the box go together in a certain way. Choose the number that goes where you see the question mark.

8, 2	12, 3	16, ?

A 3   **B** 4   **C** 8   **D** 12   **E** 16

38.

The drawings in the boxes go together in a particular way. Which drawing goes where the question mark is?

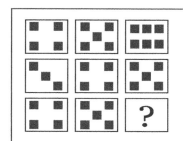

A   **B**   **C**   **D**   **E**

39.

Which number comes next in the series?

0   ½   1   1 ½   2   2 ½   ?

A 3   **B** ½   **C** 3 ½   **D** 2   **E** 4

40.

The opposite of *purchase* is _____.

A buy   **B** sell   **C** bid   **D** discount

41.

Kim baked 3 batches of cookies. Each batch had 12 cookies. How many cookies did she bake altogether?

A 4   **B** 15   **C** 36   **D** 30

42.

The figures in the boxes below relate to each other in a particular way. Which figure from the answer choices belongs in the box with a question mark?

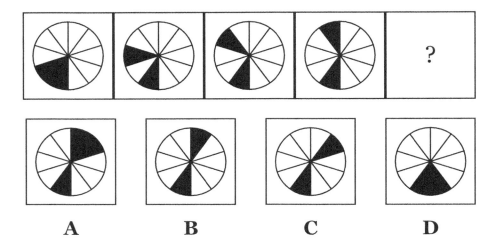

   A   **B**   **C**   **D**

43.

football : field as tennis :

A ball   **B** track   **C** ring   **D** court

44.

Which word does *not* go with the others?

A dog   **B** cat   **C** beaver   **D** rabbit   **E** hamster

45.

The figures below relate to each other in a particular way. One of them doesn't belong. Which figure does not belong with the others?

| A | B | C | D | E |

46.

All plants must have _____.

A roots   **B** flowers   **C** pollen   **D** fruit

47.

The words in the box go together in a certain way. Choose the word that goes where you see the question mark.

increase	valley	conflict
decrease	mountain	?

A struggle   **B** truce   **C** war   **D** distress

48.

Which words best complete the sentence?

Pablo was _____ with the grade on his spelling test because he had _____ the material.

A happy, forgotten   **B** distraught, solved   **C** fearful, aced   **D** satisfied, studied

49.

The drawings in the boxes go together in a particular way. Which drawing goes where the question mark is?

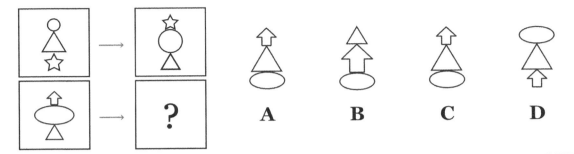

A   B   C   D

50.

If the words below were arranged to make the *best* sentence, with which letter would the **first** word of the sentence begin?

| a | achieve | to | assessment | the | good | want | grade | on | I |

A T   **B** W   **C** I   **D** A

51.

The numbers in the box go together in a certain way. Choose the number that goes where you see the question mark.

54	52	50
49	47	45
44	42	?

A 50   **B** 55   **C** 49   **D** 40

52.

The numbers in the box are related according to the same rule. Given this information, which number fits where the question mark is?

| 11, 18 | 1, 8 | 9, ? |

A 54   **B** 15   **C** 7   **D** 16   **E** 12

53.

The drawings in the boxes go together in a particular way. Which drawing goes where the question mark is?

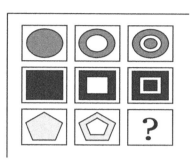

A   **B**   **C**   **D**   **E**

54.

Which number comes next in the series?

    4   0   8   0   12   0   ?

A 13   **B** 0   **C** 14   **D** 16   **E** 32

55.

The opposite of *complex* is _____.

A concave   **B** difficult   **C** simple   **D** fair

56.

Lila is saving up for a new board game that costs $12. If she earns $6 a week for doing chores, how many weeks will she need to save before she can buy the video game?

A 2 weeks   **B** 6 weeks   **C** 1 week   **D** 10 weeks

57.

The drawings in the boxes go together in a particular way. Which drawing goes where the question mark is?

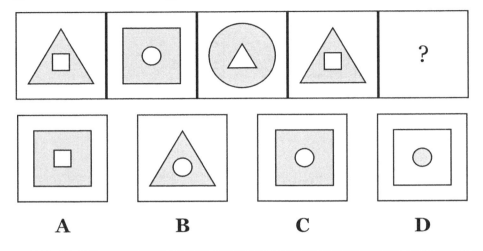

A   **B**   **C**   **D**

58.

cotton: fabric as gold:

A   scarf   **B**   metal   **C**   umbrella   **D**   saucepan

59.

Which word does not go with the others?

A   drawing   **B**   chalk   **C**   pencil   **D**   marker   **E**   crayon

60.

The figures below relate to each other in a particular way. One of them doesn't belong. Which figure does not belong?

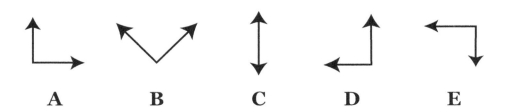

A   **B**   **C**   **D**   **E**

61.

The shapes in the top boxes go together in a certain way. Which shape belongs where the question mark is?

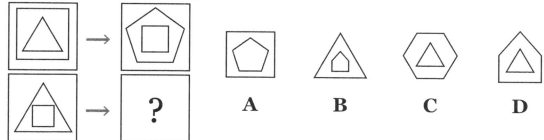

62.

The shapes in the top boxes go together in a certain way. Which shape belongs where the question mark is?

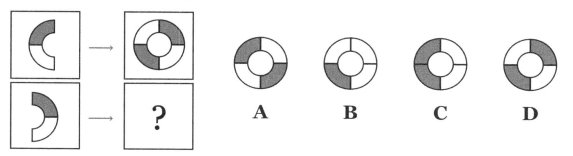

63.

The figures below relate to each other in a particular way. One of them doesn't belong. Which figure does not belong?

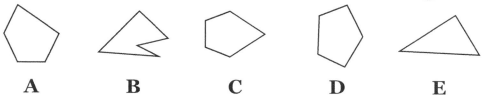

64.

The figures below relate to each other in a particular way. One of them doesn't belong. Which figure does not belong?

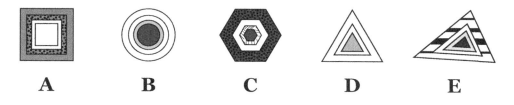

OLSAT® Level D
Practice Test 2

1.

All birds have _____.

A talons   **B** fur   **C** wings   **D** webbed feet

2.

The words in the box go together in a certain way. Choose the word that goes where you see the question mark.

be	bt	beet
bo	bk	?

A bet   **B** boot   **C** book   **D** beak

3.

Which words best complete the sentence?

Since Valentina felt _____ on stage, she forgot the words she was supposed to _____.

A confident, say   **B** apprehensive, recite   **C** comfortable, speak   **D** bored, understand

4.

The shapes in the boxes go together in a certain way. Which shape belongs where the question mark is?

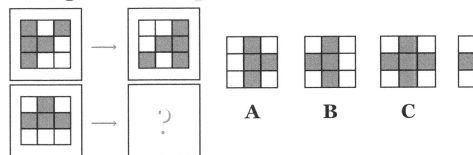

A   **B**   **C**   **D**

5.

If the words below were arranged to make the _best_ sentence, with which letter would the <u>last</u> word of the sentence begin?

decided the to arrived some not hurricane people before evacuate

A   S   **B**   P   **C**   T   **D**   A

6.

The numbers in the box go together in a certain way. Choose the number that goes where you see the question mark.

17	24	31
14	21	28
?	26	33

A   19   **B**   25   **C**   20   **D**   30

7.

The numbers in the box are related according to the same rule. Given this information, which number fits where the question mark is?

6, 60	60, 600	600, ?

A   10   **B**   6   **C**   60   **D**   60,000   **E**   6000

8.

The drawings in the boxes go together in a particular way. Which drawing goes where the question mark is?

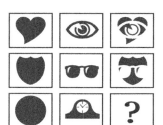

                       A   **B**   **C**   **D**   **E**

9.

Which number comes next in the series?

    10   9   11   8   12   7   ?

A 8   **B** 17   **C** 6   **D** 10   **E** 13

10.

The opposite of *exceptional* is _____.

A unique   **B** indifferent   **C** antique   **D** common

11.

Mr. Watters picked the ripe vegetables from his garden. He picked some tomatoes, 10 cucumbers, and 6 peppers. He picked 28 vegetables in all. How many tomatoes did he pick?

A 16   **B** 12   **C** 28   **D** 14

12.

The figures in the boxes below relate to each other in a particular way. Which figure from the answer choices belongs in the box with a question mark?

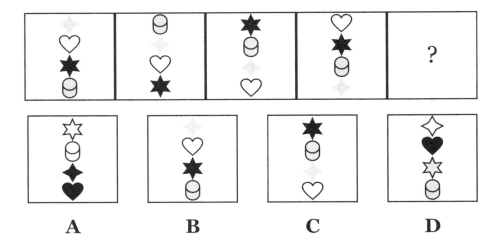

13.

desert : sand as lake :

A blue   **B** fish   **C** cactus   **D** water

14.

Which word does *not* go with the others?

A bird   **B** goose   **C** duck   **D** turkey   **E** chicken

15.

The figures below relate to each other in a particular way. One of them doesn't belong. Which figure does not belong?

  A   **B**   **C**   **D**   **E**

16.

The result of her job interview was very _____.

A positive   **B** level-headed   **C** clever   **D** excited

17.

The words in the box go together in a certain way. Choose the word that goes where you see the question mark.

onion	parachute	queen
orangutan	pineapple	?

A cantaloupe **B** gorilla **C** king **D** quiz

18.

Which words best complete the sentence?

Because he _____ his pencil, James had to _____ one from Jaxson.

A bought, donate **B** sharpened, take **C** misplaced, borrow **D** lost, find

19.

The shapes in the top boxes go together in a certain way. Which shape belongs where the question mark is?

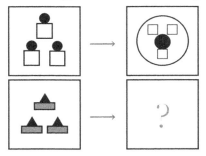

A **B** **C** **D**

20.

If the words below were arranged to make the *best* sentence, with which letter would the last word of the sentence begin?

trapeze	on	flexible	the	swing	the	fly	and	acrobats

A A **B** T **C** F **D** O

21.

The numbers in the box go together in a certain way. Choose the number that goes where you see the question mark.

35	43	51
42	50	58
48	?	64

A 57 **B** 53 **C** 56 **D** 60

22.

The numbers in each box are related according to the same rule. Given this information, which number fits where the question mark is?

6, 2	18, 6	36, ?

A 11 **B** 4 **C** 6 **D** 8 **E** 12

23.

The drawings in the boxes go together in a particular way. Which drawing goes where the question mark is?

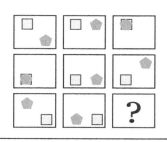

A **B** **C** **D** **E**

24.

Which number comes next in the series?

0   10   30   60   100   150   ?

A 300 **B** 50 **C** 0 **D** 175 **E** 210

25.

The opposite of *thaw* is to _____.

A freeze   **B** heat   **C** melt   **D** evaporate

26.

Rob sent out 6 invitations for his party. His mom invited 4 more guests. If Rob wants each of the invited guests to have 2 cupcakes, how many cupcakes will he need?

A 12   **B** 10   **C** 25   **D** 20

27.

The figures in the boxes below relate to each other in a particular way. Which figure from the answer choices belongs in the box with a question mark?

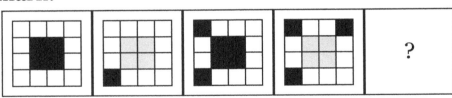

 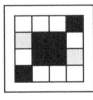 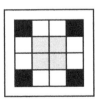

    A   **B**   **C**   **D**

28.

rowboat : oar as car :

A door   **B** road   **C** drive   **D** steering wheel

29.

Which word does *not* go with the others?

A dining room   **B** bedroom   **C** kitchen   **D** roof   **E** bathroom

30.

The figures below relate to each other in a particular way. One of them doesn't belong. Which figure does not belong?

   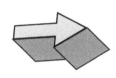

A   **B**   **C**   **D**   **E**

31.

All books have _____.

A chapters   **B** pages   **C** illustrations   **D** table of contents

32.

The words in the box go together in a certain way. Choose the word that goes where you see the question mark.

apple	egg	octopus
ape	evil	?

A over   **B** opposite   **C** octagon   **D** olive

33.

Which words best complete the sentence?

Carla used poor _____ when she was _____ to her mother about how the glass vase broke.

A sanity, truthful

B intelligence, polite

C wisdom, honest

D judgement, dishonest

34.

The shapes in the top boxes go together in a certain way. Which shape belongs where the question mark is??

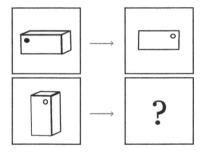

                                         A   B   C   D

35.

If the words below were arranged to make the *best* sentence, with which letter would the <u>first</u> word of the sentence begin?

water plenty flowers and grow sunlight need of to

A F   B S   C W   D P

36.

The numbers in the box go together in a certain way. Choose the number that goes where you see the question mark.

64	76	88
59	71	83
?	67	79

A 55   B 64   C 72   D 54

37.

The numbers in the box are related according to the same rule. Given this information, which number fits where the question mark is?

45, 45	100, 100	0, ?

A 100   **B** 10   **C** 0   **D** 50   **E** 45

38.

The drawings in the boxes go together in a particular way. Which drawing goes where the question mark is?

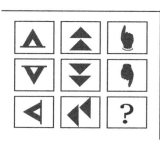

    A   **B**   **C**   **D**   **E**

39.

Which number comes next in the series?

0   5   4   9   8   13   ?

A 16   **B** 12   **C** 23   **D** 7   **E** 21

40.

The opposite of *particular* is _____.

A summary   **B** general   **C** specific   **D** section

41.

Walter visited the zoo. His favorite animals were the elephants.
How many elephants did he see if he saw 12 legs altogether? All the
elephants have four legs each.

A 12 elephants **B** 3 elephants **C** 8 elephants **D** 48 elephants

42.

The figures in the boxes below relate to each other in a particular way.
Which figure from the answer choices belongs in the box with a question
mark?

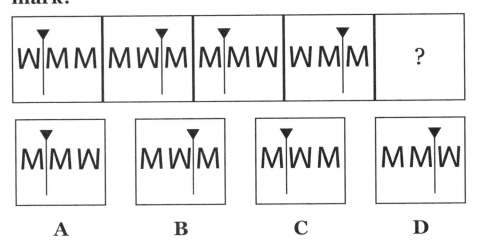

A   **B**   **C**   **D**

43.

spots : ladybug as stripes :

A leopard   **B** tiger   **C** elephant   **D** stars

44.

Which word does *not* go with the others?

A Maryland   **B** New York   **C** Florida   **D** Maine   **E** America

45.

The figures below relate to each other in a particular way. One of them doesn't belong. Which figure does not belong?

A   **B**   **C**   **D**   **E**

46.

All eyeglasses must have _____.

A   a case   **B**   lenses   **C**   glass   **D**   a prescription

47.

The words in the box go together in a certain way. Choose the word that goes where you see the question mark.

area	circumference	volume
polygon	circle	?

A   math   **B**   perimeter   **C**   rectangle   **D**   cube

48.

Which words best complete the sentence?

Because Josephine is a _____ student, she is considered more _____ than most of her peers.

A silly, mature   **B** dedicated, popular   **C** sophisticated, mature   **D** respectful, inexperienced

49.

The shapes in the top boxes go together in a certain way. Which shape belongs where the question mark is?

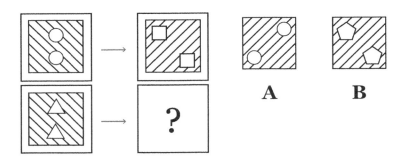

A   **B**   **C**   **D**

50.

If the words below were arranged to make the *best* sentence, with which letter would the <u>first</u> word of the sentence begin?

be supper will until all you served not your after dessert finish

A A   **B** S   **C** D   **D** Y

51.

The numbers in the box go together in a certain way. Choose the number that goes where you see the question mark.

55	66	56
50	61	51
45	?	46

A 50   **B** 56   **C** 49   **D** 40

52.

The numbers in the box are related according to the same rule. Given this information, which number fits where the question mark is?

1027, 2	4,136, 3	2,641, ?

A 1   **B** 0   **C** 4   **D** 6   **E** 2

53.

The drawings in the boxes go together in a particular way. Which drawing goes where the question mark is?

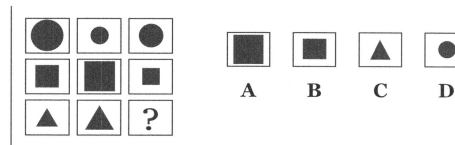

54.

Which number comes next in the series?

32   34   36   ?   40   42

A 38   **B** 37   **C** 40   **D** 48   **E** 47

55.

The opposite of *sparse* is _____.

A plentiful   **B** infrequent   **C** meager   **D** enormous

56.

The Patriots and Giants are playing each other in football. Each touchdown is worth 7 points. At the end of the game, the Patriots scored 2 touchdowns and the Giants scored 1 touchdown. What was the final score of the game?

A Patriots: 14
Giants: 7

B Patriots: 7
Giants: 0

C Patriots: 14
Giants: 21

D Patriots: 7
Giants: 14

57.

The figures in the boxes below relate to each other in a particular way. Which figure from the answer choices belongs in the box with a question mark?

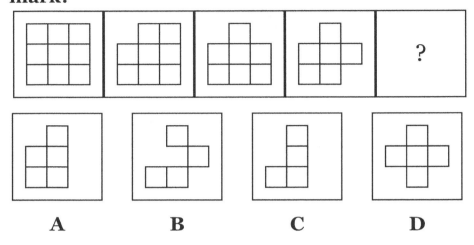

A	B	C	D

58.

rein : rain as there :

A them   **B** rare   **C** their   **D** that

59.

Which word does *not* go with the others?

A headphones   **B** earrings   **C** headboard   **D** hearing aid   **E** earplugs

60.

The figures below relate to each other in a particular way. One of them doesn't belong. Which figure does not belong?

A   B   C   D   E

61.

The shapes in the top boxes go together in a certain way. Which shape belongs where the question mark is?

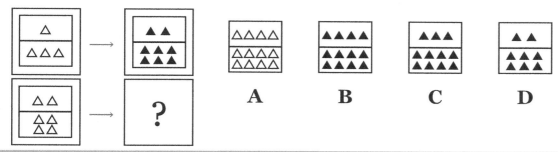

A   **B**   **C**   **D**

62.

The figures below relate to each other in a particular way. One of them doesn't belong. Which figure does not belong?

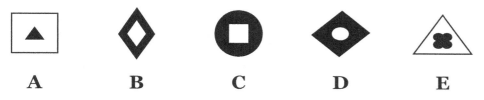

A   **B**   **C**   **D**   **E**

63.

The shapes in the boxes go together in a certain way. Which shape belongs where the question mark is?

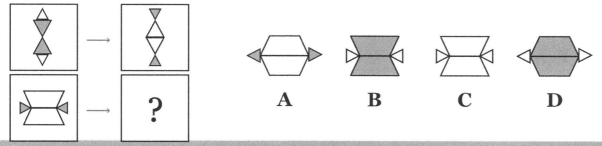

A   **B**   **C**   **D**

64.

The figures below relate to each other in a particular way. One of them doesn't belong. Which figure does not belong

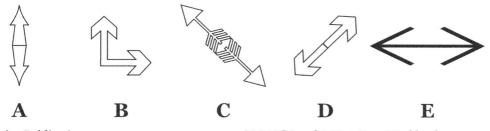

A   **B**   **C**   **D**   **E**

OLSAT LEVEL D
Answer Explanations

TEST ONE

1. **C** The correct answer is walls. Every house must have walls. A house may have windows, rugs, and stairs, but these are not necessary parts of a house. **Logical Selection.**

2. **D** The correct answer is soup. You drink juice from a cup, you eat pasta with a fork, and soup with a spoon. **Word/Letter Matrix**

3. **B** The correct answer is tripped. The phrase *because his shoes were untied* provides a clue to the missing word. The word *tripped* best completes the sentence. **Sentence Completion**

4. **D** Moving from left to right, the outer shape becomes the inner shape. In addition, the number of sides of the outer shape in the right hand box are reduced by one side compared to the left hand box. **Figural Analogies**

5. **A** The correct answer is the letter E. The sentence reads: Once the rain stopped, a beautiful rainbow emerged. **Sentence Arrangement**

6. **A** The correct answer is 59. The pattern is +14 from row to row and -11 from column to column.

31 + 14 = 45	59 − 11 = 48
45 + 14 = 59	48 − 11 = 37

Number Matrix

7. **C** Multiply by 2. **Number Inference**

8. **D** The color/shade of the outer ring alternates across the row but stays the same down each column. Across the row, the number and position of diamonds change. Down the column, the diamonds change position. **Pattern Matrix**

9. **D** Add 5 to each term in the series. **Number Series**

10. **C** *Absent* means 'not existing'. *Present* means 'being before or near a person or in sight, or being at a certain place and not elsewhere'. **Antonyms**

11. **C** If Mr Rogers ordered 8 less pizzas than Ms Coons, and Ms Coons ordered 11 pizzas, then Mr Rogers ordered 3 pizzas. 11-8=3. **Arithmetic Reasoning**

12. **D** In the first box, are three lines with black circle arrow heads. On moving from left to right, the three lines are rotated 90 degrees clockwise and dashed lines with white and black circle arrow heads are added alternatively. Therefore, in the fifth box, the three lines should face the right side and there should be 4 dashed lines with alternate white and black arrowheads. Therefore D is correct. **Figural Series**

13. **D** A candle is made of wax as a window is made of glass. **Verbal Analogies**

14. **E** The similarity among the items is that they are all punctuation marks. **Verbal Classifications**

15. **D** All are figures with six sides, except

D. Figural Classifications

16. **D** The correct answer is books. Libraries may have computers, chairs, and shelves, but these are not necessary parts of a library. **Logical Selection**

17. **B** The correct answer is *math*. In the top row, the first two items are the letters *py* and *co*. The third item is the word *copy*. You can see that the word copy is made up of a combination of the first two items, with the order reversed. The same pattern appears in the second row. In the second row, the first two items are the letters *th* and *ma*. If you combine them in the same way, it becomes *math*. **Word/Letter Matrix**

18. **C** The correct answers are *difficult* and *persevered*. 'Although' indicates a cause and effect relationship. You are looking for a word describing the math assessment which would help you determine Josie's actions while taking the assessment. The words *difficult* and *persevered* are the only words that make sense in this sentence. **Sentence Completion**

19. **D** The outer shape stays the same. Inner shapes become mirror images. **Figural Analogies**

20. **C** The correct answer is the letter S. The sentence reads: Quadrilaterals are polygons composed of four sides. **Sentence Arrangement**

21. **C** The correct answer is 47. The pattern is +5 from row to row and -2 from column to column.

$37 + 5 = 42$ $\qquad$ $52 - 2 = 49$
$42 + 5 = 47$ $\qquad$ $49 - 2 = 47$
Number Matrix

22. **B** Subtract 11. **Number Inference**

23. **A** The background color/shade and polygon alternate across and down. **Pattern Matrix**

24. **B** Subtract 6 from each term in the series. **Number Series**

25. **A** *Scarce* means lacking in quantity or number, or not plentiful. *Abundant* means existing in or possessing abundance. **Antonyms**

26. **C** If Omar gives away all of the boxes except 5 boxes, then that means he keeps 5 boxes and gives the rest (6) away. **Arithmetic Reasoning**

27. **A** In the first box is a star with an elongated arm facing upwards. On moving from left to right, the star is rotated 90 degrees clockwise and then 180 degrees. This pattern of rotation is continued. Therefore A is correct. **Figural Series**

28. **B** A dog belongs to the class of vertebrates 'mammal' as a frog belongs to the class of vertebrates called "amphibians". **Verbal Analogies**

29. **D** The similarity among the other items is that they are all <u>parts</u> of an aeroplane. **Verbal Classifications**

30. **B** All are figures with 3 shapes, except B. **Figural Classifications**

31. **B** The correct answer is plants. An

ecosystem may have fish, humans, or mountains, but these are not necessary parts of an ecosystem. **Logical Selection**

32. **D** The correct answer is *baste*. In the top row, there are the letters *ba* and *tch* followed by the word batch. The same pattern appears in the second row. In the second row, the first two items are the letters *ba* and *ste*. If you combine them in the same way, it becomes *baste*. Word/ **Letter Matrix**

33. **A** The correct answers are *strict* and *tolerate*. 'So' indicates a cause and effect relationship. You are looking for a word describing Mrs. Barry which would help you determine how she responds to misconduct. The words *strict* and *tolerate* are the only words that make sense in this sentence. **Sentence Completion**

34. **A** Shaded areas turn into unshaded areas. **Figural Analogies**

35. **D** The correct answer is the letter D. The sentence reads: A calm river meandered through the dense woods. **Sentence Arrangement**

36. **B** The correct answer is 25. pattern +3 from row to row and +3 from column 1 to column 2 and +4 from column 2 to column 3.

19 + 3 = 22	22 + 3 = 25
22 + 3 = 25	25 + 4 = 29

Number Matrix

37. **B** Divide by 4. **Number Inference**

38. **B** The number of shapes in the

boxes increase by one from left to right. Down each column, the number of shapes alternates. **Pattern Matrix**

39. **A** Add ½ to each term in the series. **Number Series**

40. **B** To *purchase* means to get an item by paying money for it. To *sell* means to exchange in return for money or something else of value. **Antonyms**

41. **C** The clue words *each* and *altogether* indicate that repeated addition/multiplication is required to answer the question. 3 x 12 = 36 cookies, 12 + 12 + 12 = 36 cookies. **Arithmetic Reasoning**

42. **B** In the first box is a circle with two adjacent parts at the bottom shaded black. On moving from left to right, the shaded part touching the middle line of the circle remains undisturbed and the other shaded part shifts one part clockwise in each step. Therefore B is correct. **Figural Series**

43. **D** Football is played on a 'field' as tennis is played on a 'court'. **Verbal Analogies**

44. **C** The similarity among the items is that they can all be common domestic pets .**Verbal Classifications**

45. **B** All are four sided shapes with two parts shaded the same color, and two parts shaded another color, except B. **Figural Classifications**

46. **A** The correct answer is roots. Some plants have flowers, pollen, or fruits, but

these are not necessary parts of a plant. **Logical Selection**

47. **B** The correct answer is *truce*. Each word in the bottom row is an antonym of the word above it. **Word/Letter Matrix**

48. **D** The correct answers are *satis ied* and *studied*. 'Because' indicates a cause and effect relationship. You are looking for an adjective that describes how Pablo is feeling that relates to his actions on the spelling test. Satisfied and studied are the only words that make sense in this sentence. **Sentence Completion**

49. **B** Middle shape gets smaller and goes to bottom. Bottom shape gets smaller and goes to top. Top shape gets larger and goes to middle. **Figural Analogies**

50. **C** The correct answer is the letter I. The sentence reads: I want to achieve a good grade on the assessment. **Sentence Arrangement**

51. **D** The correct answer is 40. The pattern is -5 from row to row and -2 from column to column.

$$50 - 5 = 45 \qquad 44 - 2 = 42$$
$$45 - 5 = 40 \qquad 42 - 2 = 40$$

Number Matrix

52. **D** Add 7. **Number Inference**

53. **B** The external shapes reflect to the inside of the larger shape. **Pattern Matrix**

54. **D** The 1st, 3rd, 5th terms in the series, etc (the odd terms) add 4. The other terms in the series - 2nd, 4th, 6th,

etc (even terms) are zeros. **Number Series**

55. **C** *Complex* means a whole made up of many complicated parts. *Simple* means free from complications. **Antonyms**

56. **A** Lila needs $12. If she earns $6 per week, she will need to do chores for 2 weeks before she can buy the board game. This problem can be solved in a variety of ways. The most efficient way to solve the problem is through a division equation: 12 ÷ 6 = 2. Students can also create a chart using a skip counting pattern.

Week #	1	2
$ Earned	6	6

Arithmetic Reasoning

57. **C** In the first box is a triangle with a square inside. All the outer shapes are grey in color and inner shapes are white in color. On moving from left to right, the inner shape becomes the outer shape in each step. Therefore C is correct. **Figural Series**

58. **B** Cotton is a type of fabric as gold is a type of metal. **Verbal Analogies**

59. **A** The similarity among the items is that they are all writing utensils. **Verbal Classifications**

60. **C** All are two arrows with right angles, except C. **Figural Classifications**

61. **A** Inner shape and outer shape each add 1 side. **Figural Analogies**

62. **A** Flip shape to mirror image.

Add same shape to create circle but with shading opposite side. **Figural Analogies**

63. **E** All are shapes with five sides, except E. **Figural Classifications**

64. **D** All shapes have 4 patterns, except D. **Figural Classifications**

TEST TWO

1. **C** The correct answer is wings. Some birds have talons or webbed feet, but all birds have wings. **Logical Selection**

2. **C** The correct answer is *book*. In the top row, the first two items are the letters *be* and *bt*. The third item is *beet*, which is a combination of the first two items. The first letter remains a *b*, the *e* is doubled, and the last letter becomes a *t*, spelling beet. The same pattern appears in the second row. In the second row, the first two items are the letters *bo* and *bk*. If you combine them in the same way, they spell the word book. **Word/Letter Matrix**

3. **B** The correct answers are *apprehensive* and *recite*. 'Since' indicates a cause and effect relationship. You are looking for an adjective that describes how Valentina feels and what happened as a result of feeling that way. The words *apprehensive* and *recite* are the only words that make sense in this sentence. Sentence Completion

4. **D** Turn shape 180 degrees (1/2 turn in a clockwise direction twice). **Figural Analogies**

5. **D** The correct answer is the letter A. The sentence reads: Some people decided not to evacuate before the hurricane arrived. **Sentence Arrangement**

6. **A** The correct answer is 19. The pattern is -3 from row 1 to row 2, + 5 from row 2 to row 3 and +7 from column to column.

$$17 - 3 = 14 \qquad 19 + 7 = 26$$
$$14 + 5 = 19 \qquad 26 + 7 = 33$$

Number Matrix

7. **E** Multiply by 10. **Number Inference**

8. **D** The shapes combine in each row from left to right to become the element in the third column. The item in the second column inverts colors when combined in the third column. **Pattern Matrix**

9. **E** The 1st, 3rd, 5th terms in the series, etc (the odd terms) add 1. The other terms in the series - 2nd,4th, 6th, etc (even terms) subtract 1. **Number Series**

10. **D** *Exceptional* means better than average. In this context, *common* means not above the average in rank, merit, or social position. **Antonyms**

11. **B** First, you need to determine how many cucumbers, 10, and peppers, 6, that Mr. Watters picked. 10 + 6 = 16. Next, you need to subtract the total number of vegetables Mr. Watters picked, 28, by the number of total cucumbers and peppers, 16. 28 − 16 = 12. This means that Mr. Watters picked 12 tomatoes. **Arithmetic Reasoning**

12. **B** In the first box is a vertical column that has a grey 4 armed star, a white heart, a black 6 armed star, and a grey cylinder. On moving from left to right, the shape at the bottom moves to the top and the other shapes are shifted down. Therefore B is correct. **Figural Series**

13. **D** Sand makes up a desert habitat as water makes up a lake habitat. **Verbal Analogies**

14. **A** The similarity among the items is that they are all types of birds. **Verbal Classifications**

15. **E** Within any figure, the shape with an even number of sides is black, and the shape with an odd number
of sides is white, except E. **Figural Classifications**

16. **A** The correct answer is *positive*. The phrase "result of her job interview' gives us a clue about the correct answer. Although a person may be described as 'levelheaded', 'clever' or 'excited' during an interview, results are not described using these words. **Logical Selection**

17. **D** The correct answer is *quiz*. Across the first row, the first letter of each of the words is *o, p,* and *q*. In the second row, the first two words also start with *o* and *p*. This means the missing word should also start with a *q*. **Word/Letter Matrix**

18. **C** The correct answers are *misplaced* and *borrow*. 'Because' indicates a cause and effect relationship. You are looking for an action that James did with his pencil and what happened as a result of this action. The words *misplaced* and *borrow* are the only words that make sense in this sentence. **Sentence Completion**

19. **C** In the top boxes, moving from left to right, 3 of the shapes (circles) become 1 larger outer shape (circle), which changes color, and 1 inner shape (circle), which remains the same color as original, but is slightly larger than the original). The other 3 shapes (squares) stay the same color, but are reflected across the horizontal axis and are slightly smaller. In the bottom boxes, moving from left to right, 3 of the shapes (triangles) become 1 larger outer shape (triangle), which changes color, and 1 inner shape (triangle), which remains the same color as original, but is slightly larger than the original). The other 3 shapes (rectangles) stay the same color, but are reflected across the horizontal axis and are slightly smaller. **Figural Analogies**

20. **B** The correct answer is the letter T. sentence reads: The flexible acrobats fly and swing on the trapeze. The sentence can also read: The flexible acrobats swing and fly on the trapeze. **Sentence Arrangement**

21. **C** The correct answer is 56. The pattern is +7 from row 1 to row 2, + 6 from row 2 to row 3, and +8 between columns.

43 + 7 = 50	48 + 8 = 56
50 + 6 = 56	56 + 8 = 64

Number Matrix

22. **E** Divide by 3. **Number Inference**

23. **B** The pentagon moves

counterclockwise while the square stays in the same corner in each row. The square and pentagon overlap once in each row with the pentagon on top of the square. **Pattern Matrix**

24. **E** Each term adds 10, 20, 30, 40, etc., progressively. **Number Series**

25. **A** *Thaw* means to become free of the effects of cold temperatures by being exposed to warmth. *Freeze* means to harden into or be hardened into a solid (like ice) by loss of heat. **Antonyms**

26. **D** First, determine how many people were invited to the party altogether. You do this by adding the number of people Rob invited, 6, to the number of people his mom invited, 4. 6 + 4 = 10 guests. Next, multiply 10 x 2 because each guest is going to have 2 cupcakes. 10 x 2 = 20. **Arithmetic Reasoning**

27. **A** In the first box is a square with 4 x 4 grids, and the middle 4 grids are shaded black. On moving from left to right, the color of these 4 grids alternates between black and grey. Also, starting from the bottom left grid, each corner grid is shaded black in each step. Therefore A is correct. **Figural Series**

28. **D** An oar is used to steer a rowboat as a steering wheel is used to steer a car. **Verbal Analogies**

29. **D** The similarity among the items is that they are all rooms in a house, except D. **Verbal Classifications**

30. **D** Only 2-D shapes, except D. **Figural Classifications**

31. **B** The correct answer is *pages*. Some books have chapters, illustrators, or a table of contents, but these are not necessary parts of a book. **Logical Selection**

32. **A** The correct answer is *over*. Each word in the bottom row contains the long vowel sound of the short vowel sound in the row above. The word *ape* contains the long vowel *a* and *apple* contains the short vowel *a*. The word *evil* contains the long vowel *e* and *egg* contains the short vowel *e*. The word *over* contains the long vowel *o* and *octopus* contains the short vowel *o*. **Word/Letter Matrix**

33. **D** The correct answers are *judgement* and *dishonest*. The word *poor* and the phrase *how the glass broke* are clues that you are looking for words that are negative. *Judgement* and *dishonest* are the only words that make sense in this sentence. **Sentence Completion**

34. **D** Large outer shape changes from 3D to 2D. Inner shape moves to opposite corner (top) and changes color. **Figural Analogies**

35. **A** The correct answer is the letter F. The sentence reads: Flowers need plenty of water and sunlight to grow. **Sentence Arrangement**

36. **A** The correct answer is 55. The pattern is -5 from row 1 to row 2, -4 from row 2 to row 3, and +12 from column to column.

$64 - 5 = 59$ $55 + 12 = 67$
$59 - 4 = 55$ $67 + 12 = 79$

Number Matrix

37. **C** Equal to. **Number Inference**

38. **D** The shapes in the top row are all pointing upwards, in the middle row downwards, and in the bottom row to the left. **Pattern Matrix**

39. **B** Alternatively add five and subtract one. **Number Series**

40. **B** *Particular* means relating to the separate parts of a whole. *General* means involving or affecting the whole. **Antonyms**

41. **B** Each elephant has four legs. This problem can be solved in a variety of ways. The most efficient way to solve the problem is through a division equation: $12 \div 4 = 3$. Students can also create a chart using a skip counting pattern.

Legs#	4	6	12
Elephant/s	1	1	3

Students could also use the guess and check strategy to solve this problem by trying each answer choice to see if it works. In order to determine the correct answers, students must multiply the number in the answer choice by 4 (the number of legs on each elephant.) **Arithmetic Reasoning**

42. **C.** The letter 'W' moves from the first to second to third position and then back to first position (ie ; the pattern starts again). Also, the position of the line with the triangular arrowhead shifts between the left and right of the middle letter. Therefore C is correct. **Figural Series**

43. **B** Ladybugs have spots on their bodies as tigers have stripes on their bodies. **Verbal Analogies**

44. **E** The similarity among the items is that they are all states in the United States, except E. **Verbal Classifications**

45. **D** All are figures with 5 sides, except D. **Figural Classifications**

46. **B** The correct answer is frames. Some eyeglasses come in a case, are made of glass, or require a prescription, but these are not necessary aspects of eyeglasses. **Logical Selection**

47. **D** The correct answer is *cube*. Each word in the bottom row is the name of a shape that can be measured using the math processes in the top row. You find the area of polygons, you find the circumference of a circle, and you find the volume of a cube. **Word/Letter Matrix**

48. **C** The correct answers are *sophisticated* and *mature*. 'Because' indicates a cause and effect relationship. You are looking for a word that describes Josephine and how she compares to her peers. The words *sophisticated* and *mature* are the only words that make sense in this sentence. **Sentence Completion**

49. **B** Inner shapes change to new shapes, and move from middle positions to outer corner edges (top left, bottom right). Diagonal stripes move in a different direction. **Figural Analogies**

50. **C** The correct answer is the letter D.

The sentence reads: Dessert will not be served until you finish all your supper. **Sentence Arrangement**

51. **B** The correct answer is 56. The pattern is -5 from row to row and +11 from column 1 to column 2 and -10 from column 2 to column 3.

$66 - 5 = 61$ $\quad\quad$ $45 + 11 = 56$
$61 - 5 = 56$ $\quad\quad$ $56 - 10 = 46$

Number Matrix

52. **C** Place Value: tens place. **Number Inference**

53. **E** The background shapes alternate between large, middle and small across and down. **Pattern Matrix**

54. **A** Add 2 to each term in the series. **Number Series**

55. **A** *Sparse* means few and scattered elements. *Plentiful* means present in large numbers or amount. **Antonyms**

56. **A** To determine the correct answer, students need to multiply the number of touchdowns each team scored by 7 (the number of points each touchdown is worth.)

Patriots: 2 touchdowns x 7 = 14

Giants: 1 touchdown x 7 = 7

Arithmetic Reasoning

57. **D** In the first box, is a square with 3 x 3 grids. On moving from left to right, the top left, top right and bottom right grids are removed in each step. In the fifth step, the bottom left grid must be removed. Therefore D is correct. **Figural Series**

58. **C** 'Rein' and 'rain' are homophones like 'there' and 'their' are homophones. **Verbal Analogies**

59. **C** The similarity among the items is that they are all products that are worn on/around the ear, except C. **Verbal Classifications**

60. **A** All inner shapes are black, and the outer shapes are white, except A. **Figural Classifications**

61. **B** Number of shapes doubles. Shapes change colors. **Figural Analogies**

62. **B** Inner shape different than outer shape, except B. **Figural Classifications**

63. **D** Two large shapes flip to create new shape and change color. Smaller shapes on outside of larger shapes flip and change color. **Figural Analogies**

64. **B** Arrows pointing opposite (180 degrees), except B. **Figural Classifications**

OLSAT D - TEST ONE

Use a No. 2 Pencil
Fill in bubble completely.
Ⓐ ⬤ Ⓒ Ⓓ

Name:_____

Date:_____

1. Ⓐ Ⓑ Ⓒ Ⓓ	23. Ⓐ Ⓑ Ⓒ Ⓓ Ⓔ	45. Ⓐ Ⓑ Ⓒ Ⓓ Ⓔ
2. Ⓐ Ⓑ Ⓒ Ⓓ	24. Ⓐ Ⓑ Ⓒ Ⓓ Ⓔ	46. Ⓐ Ⓑ Ⓒ Ⓓ
3. Ⓐ Ⓑ Ⓒ Ⓓ	25. Ⓐ Ⓑ Ⓒ Ⓓ	47. Ⓐ Ⓑ Ⓒ Ⓓ
4. Ⓐ Ⓑ Ⓒ Ⓓ	26. Ⓐ Ⓑ Ⓒ Ⓓ	48. Ⓐ Ⓑ Ⓒ Ⓓ
5. Ⓐ Ⓑ Ⓒ Ⓓ	27. Ⓐ Ⓑ Ⓒ Ⓓ	49. Ⓐ Ⓑ Ⓒ Ⓓ
6. Ⓐ Ⓑ Ⓒ Ⓓ	28. Ⓐ Ⓑ Ⓒ Ⓓ	50. Ⓐ Ⓑ Ⓒ Ⓓ
7. Ⓐ Ⓑ Ⓒ Ⓓ Ⓔ	29. Ⓐ Ⓑ Ⓒ Ⓓ Ⓔ	51. Ⓐ Ⓑ Ⓒ Ⓓ
8. Ⓐ Ⓑ Ⓒ Ⓓ Ⓔ	30. Ⓐ Ⓑ Ⓒ Ⓓ Ⓔ	52. Ⓐ Ⓑ Ⓒ Ⓓ Ⓔ
9. Ⓐ Ⓑ Ⓒ Ⓓ Ⓔ	31. Ⓐ Ⓑ Ⓒ Ⓓ	53. Ⓐ Ⓑ Ⓒ Ⓓ Ⓔ
10. Ⓐ Ⓑ Ⓒ Ⓓ	32. Ⓐ Ⓑ Ⓒ Ⓓ	54. Ⓐ Ⓑ Ⓒ Ⓓ Ⓔ
11. Ⓐ Ⓑ Ⓒ Ⓓ	33. Ⓐ Ⓑ Ⓒ Ⓓ	55. Ⓐ Ⓑ Ⓒ Ⓓ
12. Ⓐ Ⓑ Ⓒ Ⓓ	34. Ⓐ Ⓑ Ⓒ Ⓓ	56. Ⓐ Ⓑ Ⓒ Ⓓ
13. Ⓐ Ⓑ Ⓒ Ⓓ	35. Ⓐ Ⓑ Ⓒ Ⓓ	57. Ⓐ Ⓑ Ⓒ Ⓓ
14. Ⓐ Ⓑ Ⓒ Ⓓ Ⓔ	36. Ⓐ Ⓑ Ⓒ Ⓓ	58. Ⓐ Ⓑ Ⓒ Ⓓ
15. Ⓐ Ⓑ Ⓒ Ⓓ Ⓔ	37. Ⓐ Ⓑ Ⓒ Ⓓ Ⓔ	59. Ⓐ Ⓑ Ⓒ Ⓓ Ⓔ
16. Ⓐ Ⓑ Ⓒ Ⓓ	38. Ⓐ Ⓑ Ⓒ Ⓓ Ⓔ	60. Ⓐ Ⓑ Ⓒ Ⓓ Ⓔ
17. Ⓐ Ⓑ Ⓒ Ⓓ	39. Ⓐ Ⓑ Ⓒ Ⓓ Ⓔ	61. Ⓐ Ⓑ Ⓒ Ⓓ
18. Ⓐ Ⓑ Ⓒ Ⓓ	40. Ⓐ Ⓑ Ⓒ Ⓓ	62. Ⓐ Ⓑ Ⓒ Ⓓ
19. Ⓐ Ⓑ Ⓒ Ⓓ	41. Ⓐ Ⓑ Ⓒ Ⓓ	63. Ⓐ Ⓑ Ⓒ Ⓓ Ⓔ
20. Ⓐ Ⓑ Ⓒ Ⓓ	42. Ⓐ Ⓑ Ⓒ Ⓓ	64. Ⓐ Ⓑ Ⓒ Ⓓ Ⓔ
21. Ⓐ Ⓑ Ⓒ Ⓓ	43. Ⓐ Ⓑ Ⓒ Ⓓ	
22. Ⓐ Ⓑ Ⓒ Ⓓ Ⓔ	44. Ⓐ Ⓑ Ⓒ Ⓓ Ⓔ	

OLSAT D - TEST TWO

Use a No. 2 Pencil
Fill in bubble completely.
Ⓐ ● Ⓒ Ⓓ

1. Ⓐ Ⓑ Ⓒ Ⓓ	23. Ⓐ Ⓑ Ⓒ Ⓓ Ⓔ	45. Ⓐ Ⓑ Ⓒ Ⓓ Ⓔ
2. Ⓐ Ⓑ Ⓒ Ⓓ	24. Ⓐ Ⓑ Ⓒ Ⓓ Ⓔ	46. Ⓐ Ⓑ Ⓒ Ⓓ
3. Ⓐ Ⓑ Ⓒ Ⓓ	25. Ⓐ Ⓑ Ⓒ Ⓓ	47. Ⓐ Ⓑ Ⓒ Ⓓ
4. Ⓐ Ⓑ Ⓒ Ⓓ	26. Ⓐ Ⓑ Ⓒ Ⓓ	48. Ⓐ Ⓑ Ⓒ Ⓓ
5. Ⓐ Ⓑ Ⓒ Ⓓ	27. Ⓐ Ⓑ Ⓒ Ⓓ	49. Ⓐ Ⓑ Ⓒ Ⓓ
6. Ⓐ Ⓑ Ⓒ Ⓓ	28. Ⓐ Ⓑ Ⓒ Ⓓ	50. Ⓐ Ⓑ Ⓒ Ⓓ
7. Ⓐ Ⓑ Ⓒ Ⓓ Ⓔ	29. Ⓐ Ⓑ Ⓒ Ⓓ Ⓔ	51. Ⓐ Ⓑ Ⓒ Ⓓ
8. Ⓐ Ⓑ Ⓒ Ⓓ Ⓔ	30. Ⓐ Ⓑ Ⓒ Ⓓ Ⓔ	52. Ⓐ Ⓑ Ⓒ Ⓓ Ⓔ
9. Ⓐ Ⓑ Ⓒ Ⓓ Ⓔ	31. Ⓐ Ⓑ Ⓒ Ⓓ	53. Ⓐ Ⓑ Ⓒ Ⓓ Ⓔ
10. Ⓐ Ⓑ Ⓒ Ⓓ	32. Ⓐ Ⓑ Ⓒ Ⓓ	54. Ⓐ Ⓑ Ⓒ Ⓓ Ⓔ
11. Ⓐ Ⓑ Ⓒ Ⓓ	33. Ⓐ Ⓑ Ⓒ Ⓓ	55. Ⓐ Ⓑ Ⓒ Ⓓ
12. Ⓐ Ⓑ Ⓒ Ⓓ	34. Ⓐ Ⓑ Ⓒ Ⓓ	56. Ⓐ Ⓑ Ⓒ Ⓓ
13. Ⓐ Ⓑ Ⓒ Ⓓ	35. Ⓐ Ⓑ Ⓒ Ⓓ	57. Ⓐ Ⓑ Ⓒ Ⓓ
14. Ⓐ Ⓑ Ⓒ Ⓓ Ⓔ	36. Ⓐ Ⓑ Ⓒ Ⓓ	58. Ⓐ Ⓑ Ⓒ Ⓓ
15. Ⓐ Ⓑ Ⓒ Ⓓ Ⓔ	37. Ⓐ Ⓑ Ⓒ Ⓓ Ⓔ	59. Ⓐ Ⓑ Ⓒ Ⓓ Ⓔ
16. Ⓐ Ⓑ Ⓒ Ⓓ	38. Ⓐ Ⓑ Ⓒ Ⓓ Ⓔ	60. Ⓐ Ⓑ Ⓒ Ⓓ Ⓔ
17. Ⓐ Ⓑ Ⓒ Ⓓ	39. Ⓐ Ⓑ Ⓒ Ⓓ Ⓔ	61. Ⓐ Ⓑ Ⓒ Ⓓ
18. Ⓐ Ⓑ Ⓒ Ⓓ	40. Ⓐ Ⓑ Ⓒ Ⓓ	62. Ⓐ Ⓑ Ⓒ Ⓓ Ⓔ
19. Ⓐ Ⓑ Ⓒ Ⓓ	41. Ⓐ Ⓑ Ⓒ Ⓓ	63. Ⓐ Ⓑ Ⓒ Ⓓ
20. Ⓐ Ⓑ Ⓒ Ⓓ	42. Ⓐ Ⓑ Ⓒ Ⓓ	64. Ⓐ Ⓑ Ⓒ Ⓓ Ⓔ
21. Ⓐ Ⓑ Ⓒ Ⓓ	43. Ⓐ Ⓑ Ⓒ Ⓓ	
22. Ⓐ Ⓑ Ⓒ Ⓓ Ⓔ	44. Ⓐ Ⓑ Ⓒ Ⓓ Ⓔ	

Made in the USA
Coppell, TX
17 March 2020